Heat Lightning:
New and Selected Poems
1986 – 2006

Heat Lightning:
New and Selected Poems
1986 – 2006

Judith Skillman

Silverfish Review Press
Eugene, Oregon

Publication of this book was made possible in part by a generous grant
from Literary Arts of Portland, Oregon.

Published by
Silverfish Review Press
P.O. Box 3541
Eugene, OR 97403
www.silverfishreviewpress.com

Distributed by
Small Press Distribution
800-869-7553
orders@spdbooks.org
www.spdbooks.org

Library of Congress Cataloging-in-Publication Data

Skillman, Judith, 1954-
    Heat lightning : new and selected poems, 1986-2006 / Judith Skillman.
-- 1st ed.
       p. cm.
    ISBN 1-878851-23-3
    I. Title.
PS3569.K483H43 2006
811'.54--dc22
                                         2005036297

Contents

New Poems

Hats Off

Judith Skillman's poetic career opens with a soft punch to the gut. In the first poem of this collection of new and selected work, she writes of learning that an unborn child has arrhythmia and speaks of "staring blankly into the future / as though it were written in chimney smoke." Two pages later, though, she's cracking jokes in "The Librarian Decides On Cryonics" when she says, "Hats off, then, to the librarian, / his head, that is, strapped in a steel urn / in a one-way glass building, / catalogued and paid up through 2200."

These two very different poems are from her first book, *Worship of the Visible Spectrum* (1988). By *Beethoven and the Birds* (1996), Skillman is bringing the tragic and the comic together in poems like the aptly-titled "The Queen of Fatigue."

Most poets would stop there. Many of us have a couple of different tricks we learn early, and at some point it occurs to us that, if we combine everything we know, the result will be a whole that's more than the sum of its parts.

Yet as the books continue to accumulate, you can see Skillman testing herself and discovering new ways of tempering her words. "Tic Douloureux," from *Storm* (1998), is close to being a L=A=N=G=U=A=G=E poem: "The trigger is sensation. / The violin's a dirty animal." Within the same collection, though, "Rookery" goes in the opposite direction. It's almost conversational (it begins "I too have an Uncle Jake"), as is "Sad Breed" ("My father meant to be kind when he cussed") (*Red Town*, 2001).

Reader, I could walk you through this sumptuous book, drawing your eye to one stunning effect after another. But why linger over my prose when you should be tripping eagerly towards the myriad pleasures of Judith Skillman's poetry? By the time you get to the new work, you will, as I did on reading, say, "Porch Light," feel fortunate to have spent these hours with a poet who knows every trick in the book yet never lets on that she's doing anything other than saying what's in her heart and now yours as well.

—David Kirby

Schematic Nocturne

Fennel, serpent and rush.
Aroma, scent and penumbra.
Air, earth and solitude.

(The ladder reaches to the moon.)

Federico Garcia Lorca,
Primeras Canciones
translated by Stanley Read

for my family — Tom, Drew, Jocelyn,
Lisa & Josh

From Worship of the Visible Spectrum (1988)

Written on Learning of Arrhythmia in the Unborn Child

I would liken wood smoke to death
except for the birds which pass through
and emerge intact, and the sky that stands
quietly behind it, white with the chance of snow.

The horse made out of yesterday's snow
loosens its stone eyes and sculpted mane.
In time it will lose everything
except the brave forelegs, those it never had.

I could go on watching these things
until nightfall, which comes each evening
earlier now. I would sit in the inner dark
of a suburban house that burns with life,
my other children lit from within
by ivory bones and papier-mâché complexions.
Their blood flows easy as candle wax
melted from crayons.

I could stay here in the warm pocket
that precedes shock, unlike those women
who don't feel their own faces
anymore. They walk from room to room
in the four, perfect chambers
of their own hearts,

staring blankly into the future
as though it were written in chimney smoke,
carrying the past in their striated laps.
Listen as they mouth the name of the child
that was meant to be, while around them
silence widens, and the depths.

Study in Blue

That portion lying between green and violet,
filling in around long-stemmed trees
that line the avenue. The pale cloth
of distance, fractured with birds.

There is nothing the bluing would not have:
it reaches in with the five possible
shadings of light, Chinese brushes
sweeping back and forth without thought.

The road wears an asphalt signature,
as everything becomes more
of what it already was: fleshed out forms
of circles and cylinders.

To draw this
you need a mind that can deepen,
irreversibly, as the sky does
before solstice, when dusk
takes so long to quiet the outlines
of trees.

Doves take over the cherry,
gray in the measure of their devotions.
Pairs for whom happiness is the white flowers
before, and the only sound worth making
is one that fills this landscape
and the others which go on around us,
empty, emptying.

The Librarian Decides on Cryonics

Just his head, stuffed with children's books
and the thin yellow cards of the catalogue,
tissue ruffled and scored with red letters
of microfiche. Right and left halves,
aisles where the bad novels grow worse
and the good novels go unread.

And not that it was easy to make this decision,
when he met the cryologist at a party.
It was doubt and mixed drinks, the cherry
of the lush present dangling on its thin stem
into their glasses. Just talk.

That's when the books reached into his life
with their thin jackets and took his loved ones,
one by one, a father, an aunt, the grandmother
whose jellies well-deserved their local reputation.
It became obvious, the fragility of life,
the slim volumes filled with their choices:
die or be frozen, freeze-dried.

He'll have a new body though. It's expensive
to freeze a body, one so footnoted with cancer
and bad vision as his will be.
Hats off, then, to the librarian,
his head that is, strapped in a steel urn
in a one-way glass building,
catalogued and paid up through 2200.
With all the time in the world to kill,
and the entire backlog of the humanities
to take his time on, thawing out and catching up.

Worship of the Visible Spectrum

This is the light
which, like a sudden stroke of fortune,
finds itself lodged in a particular flower.
Take the primrose, hardy
as a crystal. Then we love the saturation point
of petals, and celebrate the specific,
like the child with his primary colors,
each one thick enough to stay put.

Or this light is merely the lightness of birds,
an adjective. Cheerful, but holding no opinion
on the matter of flight. Unconcerned.
As by some miracle the red-headed parrot finch
invests its feathers in every range
of the visible spectrum. This makes it rare,
forbidden for export.
A probable victim of poachers and extinction.

There are other birds, so brilliantly hued
they are labeled "problem birds."
Nervous and shy, they crave
privacy and drop dead in captivity for no apparent reason.
There is no way to guarantee
that they will breed.
To them the light is everywhere,
a frivolous interruption, a lack of dark.

Yesterday the sun fell into my son's bowl
like a bird he chose to save.
To him windows are yet prisms,
leaving approximate rainbows on the walls.
Night requires a twenty-five watt bulb,
and the chicken he lost to the dogs
still carries its soul, a few yellow feathers
wrapped in a baggie.

Anything is possible.
Wind could be light, except that leaves
don't carry in a vacuum.
I still have much to explain to them—
infra-red, ultra-violet, the force fields
around the blind. My children draw x-rays
of their hands on white paper as we pass the equinox,
and the visual purple of crocus begins.

Afternoon of the Child Genius

She can make anything out of anything,
tailor with a sharp needle,
gardener with a green thumb.
Things turn out best on the floor
when, legs splayed out beside her,
she whispers to herself about wing sizes
and the longings of small animals for shelter.

Through her hands I see the sky,
acres of the same blue fabric trimmed
with lace. The clouds are a running stitch.
Every letter is there, ready to be drawn,
planted, or appliquéd.
She knows how to fashion bear blankets,
the purse of the monkey, the pillow
the clay snail will use when every drop
of water is gone.

To say that she dreams in color
would be unfair.
The colors migrate toward her
in every saturation and hue,
they play out like compliments and spare suns.
Even the beaks of her stuffed birds
have gone from orange to the heart of orange.

Star Map With Two Lovers

We have had this argument before,
turned our wheels
over the empty driveway.
But we come back,
because the two lovers
are still there
under the umbrella of their vast planetarium.
Cephus and Cassiopeia,
her foot light years away from his shoulder.

They are making love
with their approximate hips.
Speeding away and together again,
maybe sixteen times since the beginning
of time, if you believe the theory
of the pulsating universe.
Whatever theory you bank on,
remember the appearance
of finality. How night after night
we can see their argument,
their reconciliation,
the vastness of their disagreements
against the corporation of the galaxies.
Are they married
or just living together,
king and queen of astronomical lust.

See how he wines and dines her,
oblivious to the blank spaces in her wrists,
her boundless yearning, the pulsar
in her apparent neck.

From Beethoven and the Birds (1996)

A Conceit

While doing laundry
a woman finds a fragment of music
stuck like pitch
to a shirt, and begins to swab
in circles with her bristly brush,
but the pitch is stubborn—
it coats her hands.

When she goes to wash them
she finds herself
rooted to the floor
like a willow, utterly graceful,
her hands welded
to bronze faucets.

She notices dark wings
brushing against her face—
the hair of a younger woman,
but who?
If she could turn her head
she is certain she would recognize
the figure.

Deep in the recesses of her shoulders
she feels warmth, and now the sun
has broken through the window
as though it too
wants to return her
to her life.

Tinnitus

All night the woman floats
in her twin bed, hearing the wind
whoosh, the rain slap and beat
against shutters. She has given
everything to find this white river,
where she can stand and see the glacier
move its snout along a ridge, nosing
the ground as it uproots trees
and sends rocks to their death.

But rocks can't die, she thinks,
as wind and rain pour ceaselessly
through her. She supposes the past, like matter,
can be neither created nor destroyed.
And as she sleeps she rummages
through shells on a beach, touching feathers
that murmur like birds, looking
for her lost ring. In her dream she hears
the common crow chase a red-tailed hawk
into a corner of the sky.

Beside her bed the ocean roars
its single name, coursing
from the sound conditioner.
A light rain thrums. Wind choruses
its white noise, wakening
vibrations deep within her cochleae.
She hears her mother's fine china
shiver from a shelf and break.

The Fingerboard

Inside the circle
of my hand are hermits
with lifted pincers.
Their borrowed
houses blacken.

A secret,
the ebony gives.
Under the new
order there's a rush
on glass figurines.
When I crush them
I hear the pop of gristle,
sound of a broken nose
or a statistician
counting the odds.
I can't believe how tiny
the numbers, how delicate.

And this is only a sampling
of superstructures
it took centuries to build.
I coax shellfish
out of the middle ear.

One doctor reported
cutting through bone stays
with a knife, to release
the hordes of ladies
who fainted in public.

I stomp
the exact center
of each note
in order to approach

even one of the deformed angels
with its fear
of flowers and numbers.

Gourds

Because they are essentially useless
except for decoration, I think of them
again tonight while you sprawl on the couch
in TV snow, sleep off another difficult day
that began too early, light breaking through
your privacy window to spread its fan.
    They are virtuosos
of variety—dawn, our love life, these gourds.
I am lifting foliage like a skirt, to determine
what it was worth, our arguments over money
and the child; the harsh armor you've amassed
these recent months. What for?
And how beautifully conceived, I want to say,
both remarks framed with flowers.

Their dimpled cups of scent
are not more surprising than the stage-black veins
of the eggplant, whose hidden domes are comelier,
more regular, than the oversexed gourds.
Here and there next season's ornaments
have found a niche too early, inserted
their fruits between wires meant to train vines.
The same old round peg in a square hole, cinched
        as if it were flesh,
with a second waist squeezed from nothing.
The fence itself cycling around,
masking an unsightly sewer from visitors.

    If I stand again, in memory, before
this shrine, where the inedible fruit
meets its purpose and begins to thrive, white-
        skinned among so many broad-
leafed versions, or cave in cartoon-like, and learn to
        face abandonment
while the moon hides beneath leaves of darkness,

and shines there, will there be a way to ease sleep
away from its next victim?

Next door a blue light kills insects all night,
with a sound so regular it's almost comforting.
And I know you will wake up
close to morning, turn off the TV, and come upstairs.

How you will arrange your body between the sheets.

The Housewife Dreams of Order

They say a spray of lavender
hung upside down in a closet,
they say lemons. But she
knows better. She lets

the old screen off its hook
and stands clear. There,
it is morning. It is morning,
and noontime, and evening again

yet she has not moved.
She is planted squarely
in the space of their comings
and goings, she is waxen

and broad leafed, her shoulder
blades oiled as a fine wood,
her mind swept clean.
Nothing moves in her, no

shadows upon the triangle
of her throat and neck,
no kerchief. The wind is a rosin
that plays her hair.

The Queen of Fatigue

I wasn't feeling anything when the queen
of fatigue began her dance of tercets, reeling me
in like a big fish on a spinner. She was decked out

in ribbons that curled of their own volition—
no shears opening and closing the shark's
        noncommittal grin, no blade held over
the scene of gift-giving.

No, she was just what the doctor ordered: plenty
of rest, knowing full well that rest doesn't equal
sleep; that the dreams of those who can't lose consciousness

begin in the full light of a kitchen, and gradually
take on color, mystery, what-you-will, deepening
to hallucination. I wasn't averse to her presence,

just feeling my way between the boulders
of moments when she happened to be, as if by her
        being exact enough
I'd later think to replicate her studded face, her
        blue garters stocked

with big and little fish—those we used to consider
        too small to keep, too large to throw back
        without regret. Her face
had been leeched by crystals of rock salt. Her blush
        was taken from a stone.
She didn't speak, except as the cheap trick

of a painter who stoops to get the impression
of frost, bare as paper, against the broken window
pane of a barn. Her legs were

twice lovely, plump and sinewy as egrets.
A kingfisher defined her collarbone,
bent like a bow, primed to dive. As I wasn't doing anything

to keep her at arm's length, to this day she hides
between chinks in the dock, declares her ownership
over poles that light my path, each lamp a gull

bright enough to lose its shadow to midday sun.

Bird in the Attic Window

In the mind of the quilt maker
all things can be divided,
the foreign bird clasping
its second branch in crooked hands,

the pasture land beyond
a list of silos, an echo complete.
The symbol for flower,
whispered again, becomes a heart

or a star. The frame we desire
contains a sill so deep
that to lean into it
is to grasp softness

with our arms, or else
fall. To obtain these effects
a woman has purchased
the same bird many times.

She has notched its beak
into tissue with a wheel of teeth,
and backed out of her dreams
in order to leave the bird whole,

listening awake to its refusals,
seeing its clothing of feathers.
She would be happy
to stroke its head

before the fire, after
her cooking is finished,
when the blueberries have been
transplanted from one cold spot

to another.
The knots that hold her, *war-bride,*
bag-balm, are just tokens,
but there is no better rest,

no better place to lay her damaged hands.

Beethoven and the Birds

Walking from the lukewarm waters of the Danube
to a small door cut in history
he pauses near handfuls of tiny birds
set like bombs in the bushes and trees
bordering the baths.

          Opening
the door because now they are reduced
to notes he can't hear over the buzzing
of his own ears.

Verbless birds.
Husked notes.
Skeletal birds,
birds of procrastination,
song of the loneliness of many women
not yet translated into one...

The sight of yellow and red bars,
green bellies moot against the bark
of winter trees stops him short.

And no, this never happened.
There were no birds of this ilk near the Danube.
His home away from home
was less private than a trail I walk
afternoons, cedar swath
set back from substantial houses.

       His bear shape wanders off
on a tangential path with slow, unhurried power
and I climb into bed between layers of flannel,
not wanting to hear anymore.

The Vagaries of Fishes

After they passed beneath us I could tell
more would be coming, beneath the sand,
under the bejeweled sky, under the first
layer of earth where water exists
in flutes and eddies. I lay there with you,
not wanting to leave your side even
for them, the miraculous creatures of sex
and sediment, the ones who obey currents
and ladders, blindly seeking out their own
individual deaths, their pink flesh peeling
against the rocks. I saw the spool of eggs,
endless possibilities that would not be.
How they labored to breathe the air that night,
caught under our queen-sized bed, the male
and the female, Silvers and Kings whose pale
eyes saw into the lidless dark. I could tell
they loved each other without speech, circling
there apart from water, and I remembered
a snippet from a French film in which a woman
masturbates with a fish,
and thought how progressive
I had become in retrospect. There we were,
left behind by the tides, deserted by
the institution of wind on a night
so soundless it could have been our first
night together, before we became victims
of those slippery, dirty, messy words.

From Storm (1998)

Tic Douloureux

The trigger is sensation.

The violin's a dirty animal.

I want you to take away the suddenness.

Pain up the side of my head.

I'll have my teeth extracted one by one.

See if it makes any difference.

Rehearse for the real.

Be either present or absent.

I'll let my fingers drum ebony.

Thinking makes it worse.

I'll take the beat inside myself

and feel it up the center of my body.

A string through my head.

Imagine a hand pierced through the center by a wire.

I won't refer to Jesus or the crucifixion.

No blood in this exercise.

Let the hand move freely up and down this wire.

I'll wipe my nose when the bow

comes toward my face.

My head itches during the Vitali.

Lightning finds a way to enter the earth.

It's a pity music rises and falls.

Hide these bolts in a rock.

Insects carve sand trails as they enter the crab's eyes.

The thing of death is the animal knows when it's happening.

Leave a relic.

Any kind of pain.

Asylum

A flutter of notes,
the *tic-tic* of beak on wood, and
a red-headed woodpecker tapping, knocking
at the door of a madrona,
looking for grubs.

Come in, I say.
Enter the tree, a feminine quantity.
Penetrate the mystery of daughterhood.

Always the soft fluff of forgiveness.
Always before or after a war.
In a deep wood flooded with memory,
the ticking, the twitching. Eyes everywhere,
etched in the bark of madronas,
on moth wing. In the decorative motion
of flower and bush, and the water
retreating from yards of beached wood,
I recognize the neurotic impulse.

But it's not *neurosis* anymore. In one
of Freud's dreams he lost a tooth,
and that tooth is the one we must discuss,
the way it fits in the palm
like a cigarette or a pill.

Rookery

I too have an Uncle Jake
although he passed on
in the eighties. His hands shook
at the table and they were getting in the way
so my mother suggested he remove them.
In dreams the lack of a hand or a foot
proves to be no obstacle
but in real life it can be difficult
for a man like Uncle Jake
who was a nuclear physicist,
and needed to manipulate electrons,
especially those oddballs that possessed
an inordinate desire to travel from one shell
to another, deserting an otherwise happy molecule
to make hydrogen, argon, or helium.
In Styrofoam models
molecules seem stable, toothpicks hold
one ball to another,
but then there are always *sexceptions*,
which is a word I've just invented
and one Uncle Jake would've liked.
He would've laughed,
shaking like gravel
and Mother would have cackled and looked away
as the wire-haired terrier humped her leg
in their Kensington living room.
Never neutered, she'd whisper later.
Of all he said during gatherings of the clan
I can only remember
two things: *I wish I'd had more children.*
One's own dirt doesn't stink.

June

If a grown child departs, on her way
to an island so thick and green
it holds the future,
the daisies are impartial.
They can see all the way
up to heaven, and their white lashes
lengthen around plush brocade centers.
But they haven't any power
over their own lives.
He loves me, he loves me not,
petals stripped back
until the center quivers
like a spider in a torn web.
With the same heady scent,
by the hundreds, they develop
in slow motion
under the searchlight of a full moon.
Flowering was never a choice.
Eventually the cottonwood gives in to wind,
the girls grow breast buds
and the boys learn bad words.
Each year when the daisies
lean into one another
as if there were comfort
in being part of a crowd,
I hear their catty gossip
and I look forward to August,
cutting off their dry, shrunken heads
with my kitchen shears.

The Mole

Was it five years ago
I thought you would emerge
as from a depression, blinking
black pupils dilated
from darkness or drugs.
Your fur lovely and dark
against your pink face.
Your feet small and correct,
and what big hands you had,
like the wolf in a fairy tale.
A sharp nose meant for burrowing.
I learned of your whereabouts
in the garden. The grass moved
to tell me where you were. Clay
the texture of chocolate cake
because the earth was catholic
then. Your mother saved
eggshells and coffee grounds,
pollinated tomato plants,
ate fish during Lent. Let's count
the longish nails of this effigy,
claws that bear the natural
numbers: one through five.
Touching it, turning it face down
with a tennis shoe.
Oddly human, wearing the wet coat
of afterbirth. What's your poison.
Trespasser in a handsome yard
crisscrossed by turkey wire.

A Painter's Alphabet

Always
Bring
Cans to hold water,
Draperies,
Even light.
Full bouquets
Given already
Have potential as landscapes.
If you
Just
Knead their dry heads
Long enough
Mint will flower.
Nobody has to know
Or care if among your
Props your carry
Quilts,
Rainstripes,
Salt.
Trees might be
Understated, shaded
Versions of
Water within the long
X of perspective,
Yours, or
Zeus'.

Child

They've gone and left you alone
with the empty beds and chairs,
the yellow Formica table a clean sweep,
standing on four legs
like an animal. Left you alone in this house
that lacks a foyer. Left you to yourself,
a child enveloped in the scent
of flowers sweating
close to the earth, a child who labors
to cross a small distance
like a potato bug, lacking the hard shell
of the bug and the instinct.
What was the child to learn
with its kindergarten fingers,
its kindergarten mind? That before
they left for the movies, grown-up
women clicked their high heels,
made up their lips and blotted them with tissue.
You fish one square of toilet paper
out of the trash. What can you say
to those red lips? What the disembodied
say when they talk to one another.

Storm

He crawled into the pastoral
from the creek bed
and crossed a muddy stream
jumping like a fish,
exclaiming his own personal hallelujah's—

Shit.

There were stars
on earth too, networks
taller than he was,
and cattails patterned
a bronze field.

*

The tic, the blink.
Bad words under pressure.
They live sordid lives.

Fuck.

An endearment, almost.
Turned on its side,
a curse.

*

Then to understand
his love of storms.
The anvils
spreading out,
the synapses lightning
bridged, zig-zag.

Streaks discharging
their debits
in the great cathedral
of blacked-out cities
lit for an instant
by the grand culprit—electricity.

*

Inside our houses
we keep alive
the fear of water and heights.
Of certain colors and women.
The fear of spiders and numbers
and peanut butter.
The fear of fear—a disease
of idolatry.

*

To come by degrees
to the matter,
a fallen tree blocking the trail
like a corpse.
To learn forgiveness

as if it were a matter
of making such distinctions:
tufted titmouse, wren, swift,
and the barometer bird,
his mascot.

*

Grasses steam near the farm.
He leans into the eyepiece,
the comet stretched taut as a scar
in morning twilight.
Sirius, the dog star, blazing
as it does in time of famine.

*

I want to stitch grasses shut,
seam rushes
near the rookery.
His head's swathed
in the black hood
like a bird. He swears
under his breath
at the machinery
of the family,
these constellations
that litter the sky.

*

In one a queen
lies on her side
seducing kings.

*

What sap,
what precious solder
holds the story together—
god the original father,
witness of planets, stars, and quasars.

Eater of soups
and exotic chocolates,
purveyor of salami and smoked meat.

In foreign delicatessens
an army of large women
waited on him.

The child who thought the world
was a clap of thunder,
an errant wire,
an antennae,

an insect buzzing,
let that child
remain in hiding.

*

Women from the old country took his order,
stood over their black bottom pots
coaxing broth to a hard boil.
He sat and ate his fill, drank

the teetotaler's cup.
Sidled back out into the street
and words spilled
from the hole in his face.

*

Who smothered the air,
drank from a pewter cup?

Who came later,
at the aftermath of the age,
clothed in ceremony?

If there was softness in him
it wasn't the familiar kind.
Above his head,
his craned neck,
eclipsing binaries.
One young star
intervening
on behalf
of another. One
would-be planet's
pocked-marked face
unmasking the sun's eruptions
around the edge
of a pink moon-disc.

*

Like a stroke
of summer lightning
he stands in the grass
near the Rose of Sharon.

Compass card, variable star,
the rosette on a shoe—
flowers exist
for the sake of reminder.

The hand mower
leans against a shed,
and lightning bugs turn on-off-on
serrated green bellies.

Ornamental Plum

What was said in anger that day,
and passed between the two lovers
who lie separated by time and distance
unravels slowly
as this tree does,
facing its portion of sky and water.

It owes so much to fruitlessness.
To the wind moving coldly
between branches,
the lamps and cars
winding along the freeway,
and the nothing new that can be said
about Spring or love.

Blossoms will slip from stems
and it will be summer again,
green leafing in between houses,
lengthening days. Whether the lovers
want to be stung by *yes* or *no,*
the tree stages its flowering
beside a road.

Because to be beautiful is the same,
but not quite, as forgiven.

From Red Town (2001)

Bourne

When the Cherry
rustles above her head
she hardly realizes
why she leaves
her clothes on the rocks,

passes a hand absently
through water
as if smoothing
an infant's forehead.
Instead she takes the fruit

pressed into her hand
and watches the bloody stone
wet her fingers.
Wasn't sweetness always
a symbol for their falling.

She walks with the man
along the river bank
until they come to know
the sore places
in the soles of their feet,

the fish knifing away.
Under the currents
every death moves in time
towards them,
each cliché is soothed

into language
as if there were
no way to limit
Paradise, other than
this that has already happened.

Red Town

Maybe where I live.
The prostitute posing in a window
in Amsterdam,
that evening when I walked with my uncle.
He wanted to show her to me.
Not coal dark.
There is a woman in a red dress
and black-laced boots
who sits on a metal chair
above ground.
The starch is dry.
This miner's wife, stranded on the earth.

Parkinson's

A slowing in the nerves.
Spurred by the bony moon
and one star, an eternal nun
whose face she remembers,
she stares up at a planet
covered in mist.

The dogwood's grown so tall
she can no longer touch the flowers
that float there. At the crown
of the magnolia a few blossoms
remind her of objects
the crows could pick up and carry
if they weren't sleeping in ink.

She knows how want peels back.
Under want is numbness,
and beneath that the pity
that traps her with its color,
bright and artificial.

Huge petals float below the ceiling
of sky, its rim of cities.
Along her spine a trunk
of wood lies superimposed,
thickening with the years.

A little less dopamine left now
to cushion the urge for sex or sleep.
She wants to believe in the clear border
that might still exist
between moon and bone,
planet and star, star and flower.

Jupiter

Even though none of the old charms
work anymore, I can still walk out
under this swollen star
rooted in the sky over suburbia.
It takes its place in a landscape
swept of constellations.
Now that there are no more
stories, and no reason
for the sadness, the pills, or the quarrels,
it shivers, and its metallic light
travels a long way
to bring me news.
The tallest firs have been decapitated,
cut into logs and sold.
If a body lies buried
between the pruned skyline
and the heavens full of talk,
no one needs to know.
If I turn away from the stars
I used to name, drain elixir
from a glass, if sugar burns
to a crust on the stove
while I stand in the yard cursing,
if they call me a *Wiccan*
because I refuse to swallow any more science,
still this star will shine until it sets
in a dry pocket beside the earth
and lies hidden with the others.

The Great-Tailed Grackle

You'll ask me
what was the great-tailed grackle like?
Its shiny feathers covered in black cloth,
with the sea before and behind it,
the surf pounding as if beheading

another clump of kelp.
I'll tell you everything about that day
but only if you listen to the muted voice
of the ocean playing with brush umbrellas,
the roots of the palm lying

like a nest crumpled against the sand.
Its feathers reams of black cloth,
it was not funereal, though we were in a land
more foreign than sleep.
Perhaps this bird represents my father,

the would-be conductor
who wore a tuxedo that waxed and waned
like anger, or my mother,
who could never show her anger,
and therefore, like the grackle,

walked stiffly across the beach.
The grackle wore the sheen of rot and betrayal,
yet its beak was always clean.
Its demeanor never changed
even when it bartered for a piece of sky,

opening its long beak,
scissoring a river from land.
There may have been parrots
in an abandoned mansion crumbling back to jungle
but the grackle was less magical than real.

It walked acutely across a narrow strip of beach.
It owned the colonies as well as the heronries.
The magpie took for itself a white belly of moon,
and from the grackle's yellow eyes
another sun has sprung.

Child Days

On the first day
an acrid square of field
grew swollen,
sewed to another
by a rille of water.

A nest bloomed in a tree
and I said, *this part is and this isn't.*
Winter can't prevent
what's hidden
from coming out.

There were sticks floating
into the mouth of the garage,
gutters full of leaves and filth.
I was going farther in
toward the birthplace of Jake

and the birthplace of Aaron,
a length of coastline
swaying in the wind.
Even for the flag of no country
stitching accrues.

Birthplace of Sarah, and Ida,
the aunts swallowed whole
by uncles, swept under
like the Three Graces
with their smiles intact.

*

Bottomed out.
Under the sleight of words
and the kiss of origins,

inside that cyst where fluid
mimics blood.

Within the nest, wanting
to float off unaware,
nomadic, to wander
under the weight of infinitives
until, restored by the power

of blank days
the other places and persons
came back to me.
A field in which a needle,
gap-toothed, looked for its thimble.

The thimble a tumbrel of weeds
and an old woman
carrying a chicken
to the wise man,
who would say

if the blood ran clean.
The separation
of milk and meat,
the thin bread, and balls
that rose or sank like fishes.

*

Grease skimmed the surface of broth
where the chicken eggs
floated, iridescent. We had organ
meat, scanty rations, tenement
houses open to the wind

that leaned in
as for Shiva.
This neighbor never left,
that one was taken,
that one arrived to sicken.

In pockets
the cutlery lies, a slave.
The nest settles
at the crotch of the tree.
Order predominates in stars and cycles.

The moon is new,
greater, lesser, swollen full.
Like women it fills
and empties and lathers
the skies.

*

The field's a square of chocolate,
impinged on in sweetness
and filth until the tooth
aches to be taken
from its hole.

The cyst's an abscess
that waits to be cleaned by a needle.
In it hair, orange-blood,
and fluid coalesce
to the point of lucidity.

The aunts are different.
They wait for the other shoe
to drop, they walk on eggs,
they season meat,
yield, entreat.

Sad Breed

My father meant to be kind when he cussed.
His cussing couldn't be helped.
The consonants had to come out,
at breakfast, lunch, and dinner, especially
when Mother served his favorite meals, pot roast
or veal stew simmered slowly
all afternoon over the gas burner.

I don't mean to be unkind to my father
by calling attention to his disease.
Kindness is a difficult thing to measure.
It could be that helpfulness
is out of order. The wind knocks
but doesn't enter, knowing
we are better off without its testy breath
in our houses.

The wild rose scratches at our walls
as if it wants to come in,
but it would bloody our sheets.
Shoes are full of odors,
and windows rattle,
but there was never a man as kind
as my father, who said *shit*.
That word *shit* he held onto like a lifeboat
in bad weather. A hatless fellow,
a short Jewish man, hissing.

Lilacs

Because they signify a life
less sterile, I twist their stems
like the woman in Eliot's *Portrait*.

Only the ones which fall and catch on long grass
can be brought into the house,
which is small and cheap and faces the sea.

A strong dose of fatigue where once was longing.
I twist lilac stems and wait for the grosbeak
to come to the fork of the tree.

Dried flowers hang near the ornament,
an umbrella for hanging pots on.
Invented by the French, I'm sure.

I twist their stems. They brown now,
May turning into June,
the beach sterile. When I walk there

I pick up pebbles and drop them back down
to hear the sound of stone on sand.
A mussel glows blue but the lilac's

tawdry blooming merely means
one kind of fatigue has passed away
to be replaced by another.

In my mouth the taste of rice vinegar.
I lean towards the crooked trunk whittled clean
and catch the scent of another aesthetic.

Compliments behoove the lady in me
to find a small start of green
somewhere in the garden.

Anything alive can be felt between the fingers.
The crows line their nests
with these kinds of straws.

The Cutter

Behind my back he stands,
wearing his skull cap
in Talmudic darkness.
The patterns laid out
on long tables, suit coats
and trousers poised
to be born. Garment maker,
cutter, would be engineer—
the blank days of the calendar
fill with arms and legs
that rise from the table
with their needs intact,
like the dead.
He thinks all this
hard work ought to earn him
safety, keep the fingers pointing
straight. What's a ghetto
but a place to put in
a sixteen-hour day, a land
of shapes skewered from nothing.
The trees keep their tweed,
and the plants have forward
motion to propel them
into flower, but he keeps
coming into the shop,
adjusting his pins
under a bare bulb
tied to a string.
The halves of his life,
quartered, come into my own,
and I turn to my cousin,
saying how beautiful it is
to live in the service
of Venus, and we wonder

what the four years
meant to him, all those
fancy men and women
stylish in the face of his dullness,
the scissors eking it out,
the blunt sun rising
in a sky sewn shut.

From Circe's Island (2003)

The Duty of Ideas

"In science the primary duty of ideas
is to be useful and interesting even more
than to be 'true.'"

Wilfred Trotter

The topographical engineer's
given name was Claude Hale Birdseye.
Birdseye, Claude Hale. U.S. topographic
engineer and first president
of the American Society of
Photogrammetry.

Suppositions can be used
without being believed. 1941.
Above the ice cream cone of Mount Rainier
he's born again in the passenger seat,
his belly full of air like the twin pontoon
of a seaplane. He talks,
to boot, with a brand new,
albeit helium-induced voice.

Not too skinny, nor too high-pitched
to be of use. Just temporary.
An interruption, a risk, a glitch
in the experiment's memory.

By the time
Birdseye, a fully-fledged
topographic engineer,
steps out and says,
"The Bird of Paradise Flower, though it
is quite serviceable for house decoration,
may fail to bloom regularly
when badly handled," he is already
falling, the chute billowing up
behind him like smoke.

Way to go, Claude. So far
there is no emotional investment
in you, as an idea or a man.
The day simply branches. A leads to B
which leads, anonymously,
to the same fowls
too ancient to fly away,
chickens with tiny wings
fastened like a cramp to their sides.

Using you this way
is artless but it leads
the scientist towards a relatively
tiny *aha*, a fresh culture,
a double kidney stain. A name
like Birdseye, Claude Hale
might even culminate,
for the experienced researcher,
in the prize of an isolated froggy's heart
beating for a half hour or so.
Tap water!
By the time
Pasteur returns, Claude Hale Birdseye
has been placed in charge of aerial surveys
of the Hoover Dam.

The day remains. Gunmetal,
egg-shell, spittle-infirm, the sky
rests in its dish like a sterile culture.
A dozen more fresh fowls succumb
in the lab. At the side of the road
the accident waits to slice
a cross-section from the life
of some specimen, i.e. grub,
if this will produce a chicken that sees
only peripherally.

Give it up, Birdseye,
you nonchalant bastard.

Were you born to your name
or did your name make you?
On a forgotten index card in a drawer
the scrawl, chicken scratch,
information bite, secret germ,
incubates. *Pasteur's research
on fowl cholera was interrupted
by the vacation.*

Ten days later, bulls-eye, an inoculation.
The topographical engineer's given
name was Birdseye, Claude Hale.

He grew up looking down at the ants
raying out from a hut of needles,
and if the landscape occurred to him
as anything other than hypothesis,
each time whatever happened happened

he moved one twig and stood back
to watch the disaster, his right eye
twitching.

The Sheers

The sheers are sweeping
back and forth, their wide hems doubled.

I remember a certain kind of light, heraldic.

Of morning not much can be said,
but evening is intimation.

Evenings at home—
how to get to the child?

The Messiah refuses to come
and even on the thick gauze
of an old-fashioned speaker
only Perry Como catches and holds a falling star.

Fishes come to erase
a pattern of sun on the wood floor,
to ease the greasy stains away
from their utensils.

From week to week I wonder
where the French have gone.
Why Scotch broom dominates.

Temptation can be said to exist, if only
in the way—a line of foam here,
a wave of scum there—
cretins consent to exit from the water,
to bask in cheap treasures
above the water mark.

Oradourian Gold

From the white face of a building
I borrowed emptiness. Poplars
turn toward sun and water,
and this despite the deadwood
lodged inside their core.

*

How is it that a tree can resemble a woman.
A narrow waist, a pelvis
that flares and carries infinity.

*

Sewing the two together
mustn't be a sentimental gesture.
Nothing tormented,
no phrases like *blood-colored shutters*
or *buried gold*.

*

It becomes possible
because of happenstance.
The alder might stand at the entrance
to a town, through gates
the telltale sounds of tanks,
the little caravan containing gold bars.
Major Dickmann, it's his absence
lets the French bicyclists perform
an ambush.

*

A *route blanche*, perhaps.

If one is merely interested
in imagination, here is the tree,
stitch-stitch, there is the town.

*

The white face of the building
insists on possibility.
Had the ambush not occurred
the village would, to this day,
be benign. The road leading
up through shops, named after
the physician-mayor,
would link butchers and bread makers.

*

If the heart is a machine
that pumps and stitches,
then sentimentality is permissible.
Not to mention blood, dirt, or shit.
Not to glorify the dead
by mentioning it was on account
of the ambush
of Major Dickmann's caravan—
three vehicles: one a lorry,
two a tank, three a motorcycle.
Grandmother massacred
in her sickness, wide awake.

*

We are given to this kind of fabric,
the past with its code words
delivered by the BBC:
it's best to pee on the other side
of the wall,
the trigger happy, ready to fire
at the slightest mention

of Germans. Fifty-four years
cut and pinked, sheared
from history can, at the slightest touch,
be returned to the original garment.

*

Metal, the most tender
of the elements, and gears.
The wheel insisting, the spindle
belonging to the original design
meant to be turned by hand.

*

In the house facing the dentist
a cauldron of soup,
lifted away from the fire
when it got too hot.
Bodies shot below the waist.
In these times not to look at,
not to be able to withstand
the crispness of pleated skirts and trousers.

*

Inside the outlines
a blue chalk writes.
Fish dart. Schematics are drawn.
Pray that we never return
to the tree, or its issue—these tissue paper
patterns floating down the Glane.

Barbed Wire

The air is starched here,
we could wash our clothes in it
and hang them out to dry. And after airing,
feather stems from comforters
would poke out

through seams of down.
Beyond the window thorns are red
but this isn't because of blood,
it's just a fact of growth. I can see
a few wild roses on their way out,

can almost taste dinner wafting
from the farmhouse down the road.
Whenever anyone comes near the goats
they stand on the roof of their house
and cry, like the babies used to do

even after we had given them
what they wanted. Tufts on their heads
were soft, but the other skull
mounted above the lean-to has horns.
Its vacant eyes only seem to see.

I like to walk so far that road
is within humming distance, then
I take out my fingers and run them
across one spindle. In a game
there is winning

but these metal flowers are twisted
almost at right angles, and markers
hang on trees like belts. Close to the path
someone has piled up rocks
from large to small. I know this is a sign

meant to be read one way,
but how precariously the berries perch
on overhanging bushes, and in what dull light
the cloth loses its trees, as though each day
we were meant to be contained.

Witches Butter

It spreads across the nurse log.
Not softly, this harsh mass
of dark fungus
that absorbs light
without malice.

Not like butter,
filling and smoothing
each crevasse, nor like a summer
that floods the lawn
to put annual flowers in order.

Nor is it possessive,
simply botanical,
a species and a category,
and, like a physicist who knows each quark
but can't deal with the vicissitudes of electrical storms,

this butter
was created by a witch.
Perhaps it was Sabbath, the demonic orgy
of midnight, the beginning
of insomnia.

It poses on the log
in order to breed, to proliferate
as Mother did
when she stirred her brew
and doled out dreams.

In competition for sun
it spreads out past the boundaries
of the log.
It can't be defined
even if Rousseau were to wander through

with his notebook,
his paranoia of the populace
who turned against him.
There are fungal longings
that want a sordid past

and there are elms that include nothing
but the namelessness
of anger, the innocence of exposure,
the perverse pleasures
of victimhood

in all its disguises.
To the pot I add these others:
witches broom, abnormal viruses, and fungi.
Witches Sabbath, where the sorcerers
of small talk met and elected

to gossip someone deeply kind
into the grave. Witch hazel,
balm I apply
as a salve
for my own inflammation.

Which is, as I'll freely admit
under inquisition,
a blend of complications,
a yellow analysis, a concoction
part ego and partial recollection.

Hand Building

There are rules:
You must not betray your medium.
If a thing wants thick walls,
make them. If the legs
of the animal are thin,
let the animal lie down, as if listening.

The slabs we fashion
are of necessity awkward, rude
as those places in cities
seen only from trains.

We roll our clay
in all directions, press the air out
like bread dough
to remind us of those short days of childhood
when we went barefoot
in the pale green grass.

Growing Her Hair

This is the moment she stands
in front of me, her hands
full of bees and ashes
or rises up again despite the lye
as full of height as a tree,
a dry boxwood.

She has washed her hair in spring water
for centuries, combed it out in the sun.
She has worshipped thistles, celandine roots,
and turmeric.

I know it is her
because the sky has burned
for months
in its mortar and pestle,
high pressures
sending the rain north,
until sword ferns crumple
and the animals seek out people,
as if there were water
in the shallower developments.

I know she has walked
in their prints, with her concoctions
of steeped walnut shells
and her slaves, her hundred strokes.
Despite her age the animals
go on giving their oils for free,

agreeing to do what must be done
in her vast shadow
that falls like a moraine
over the pitted landscape.

From Latticework (2004)

Marked

First by loneliness,
and later by the tastes
that come with the solitary life—
tea and chocolate, sugar
spooned from a canister
after granules turned into a drift
of snow, hard-packed.
You learn to scrape
leavings from the top layer,
you ration yourself, talk
to yourself about Jesus,
anything to keep the house
in place. As a singer marks
time with his voice—
one note, singular vibrato—
so you measure out a quarter,
a half teaspoon, and watch
something bitter grow
a little sweet. Only after
the kettle's screamed to itself
about boiling alone
on an element of red coils,
after the walk in the dark
down a street alternating
stars and neon. *The Church
of the Nazarene* sign buzzes
and, at the zenith, whatever
it is you haven't forgotten
or forgiven pulses. Perhaps
it's the Milky Way.
That flash—meteor
or torn retina?
Maybe the only way to tell
is to keep on walking,

talking to the God
who leant his name
to every living thing
and then withdrew it,
come winter, leaving
only the objects—
lamp and spoon—haloed.
Holding the mandolin string
down with your third finger,
ringless. You know the book
by now—whomever you call on
will have also turned inward.
Each sliver of spare light
draws back from the sky
once the clocks fall back
in their places. You secure
the locks, call for certain
strays that earlier knew
what was leftover, what
the porch light meant,
and how like a widow
a married woman
with grown children can feel.

Glosa, The Sycamore

How long will these
leafless branches carry ornaments,
thorned hollow balls, the same
refusals that fell
in Maryland autumns to rest
bell-like in memory.

For what measure of time—
what beat, what note,
mote or song-like device—
how long will these
leafless branches contain the same
refusals.

Carried by disdain,
the ornaments, thorned hollow balls.
Poor days and poorer nights
tended by heat and white sheets
where my sister and I lay tousled,
parentless on iron bunks.

We fell to Maryland autumns,
crushing leaves beneath
well-scuffed shoes.
We raked. Our hair long and unwashed,
we combed metal teeth
across commune grounds.

To rest bell-like in memory
the sycamore complements
its sister-tree, the madrona.
Bark felled in shades of burnt sienna,
read like blood for the same refusals,
and how long.

House of Moon

One ice-encrusted bough of fir
rests on the roof.
Yesterday the moon
showed the snow
to be blue, barred

and striped as Jupiter.
Tonight we beheld a yellow sky,
later grayish-blue, then
it was over, the day
with its troubled adolescence.

My daughter wished
to be blanketed and held
in innocence her whole life long.
I cherished her wish,
though it was moot.

In black and white,
a photograph developed
while I slept. I dreamt
the subtleties of deckled edges—
a cottage, a beach, a home

untroubled by myalgia.
Remember my last easy morning, all
those years I detested,
bound ball and chain
by my own children?

Cursing like Hecuba
I fill the mouths
of machines with clothes
and dishes. My chores
give rhythm and pace

to this life gone cold and childless.
And no man, wearing a carnival hat
and carrot cigarette,
will come from the snow
bearing a wooden instrument,

my French violin strung
with lost desire.

Lattice

By its milky light the sun left to grow
thin, as it had before. Afternoon. Doors
slammed shut in anger—the gate, the hedgerow
planted to take the edge off being poor.

Certain birds wintered over. They flocked,
winter behavior—across the greenway
pond heavy with rain. Turning, smocked
in holiday colors, we had our say.

Rage played out like a chess game, overtures
went unanswered. The creek swelled, slippage
took the place of safety. There was no cure.

Nests blossomed in deciduous trees.
For discourse, for conversation: pillage.
We were still married. Our marriage grew poor.

Women Embroider

Above, below, it's all the same
to a woman who has deep cleaning
left in her bones,
the tone of a certain hardwood,
the blush of granite.

Don't believe the boughs
are laden with crystalline
or that the icicles
fed by run-off from mountain streams
crenellated first at the pass.

Women aren't to be trusted.
Not your daughter, lover, or wife.
Listen to the burial
of affection. The snow
makes its hard line
apparent to the firs, driving
elk lower, dividing warm from cold.
And she is the coldest one,
the woman you married.

Dante's Nest

A few flakes fall outside
the lucent window.
If this is the house of moon
then I am only so far from Dante,

his journey to join the others
in overlapping circles.
The flakes are ancient and benign,
too small to add up.

Alone in this stray nest
behold my memorabilia—flask,
germ, thorn. The deckled edges
of my roof want to be a canvas

for some mad water-colorist
who sees into the hearts of palm,
flowers of poinsettia and bougainvillea,
virtuous leaves that masquerade as flowers.

Mimesis is sticky.
I watch my pretenses fall away.
This afternoon thirty-three cantos
tell me what Paradise is—

an incomprehensible, ecstatic light
piled on asphalt and dirt,
dim reflections
from a pall of ice.

From Opalescence (2005)

The Stone in Glass

Flintware. Tiffany had gone to Brooklyn
for custom-made pieces,
following on the heels
of La Farge.

The press of marketing *favrile*
took its toll on the man
who would later
sum up what was most precious—
petal, leaf, decanter, clapper,
the centermost portion of design.

*

That copper should adhere to glass
by the fat in animal skins.
Layers of pleats,
clear panels to see what lay beyond
the curtain of opacity.

Palimpsest made by a horse's hoof
upon a leaf
over malleable earth.

That the iridescent sun and moon
might be seen not as they were,
but as secrets.

That the rag passed over mirror
if it did not act out drama,
as in reflection, imitation, mimesis.

That patterns might be called *cartoons*.

*

Scissors eating the black line,
and numbers. Lead and copper foil,
beeswax that later
melted—Tiffany's lamps
jiggled in the presence of women and children.

*

What if glass were conditional,
a substance
neither fluid nor solid.
Under what terms
then might one surrender?

Does the curve bend sharply
where it should angle gently
as a fishing rod
bent to the weight of trout,
catfish, bottom fish, or worse?

*

Bell with no clapper,
fan that moves no air,
leaves deathless in red, orange, gold—
whether folded or pronged.

The *cat's paw*
neither man would live to see.

*

Because in time nothing seeps
to the bottom except myth.
Dionysius' cup razed by fire,
Prometheus chained to the rock again,
his liver and heart
equal to the eagle or vulture.

The talismans are endless—
sailboat, mandala, flower, stem, bell.

The stone's not in favor of comfort.
Stone in one's shoe, proverbial
soup made with cabbage and stones.
Jumars, pitons, and dead men for climbers.

Whatever is put under the knife
and does not tell.

The Speed of Light

The meter of time
was planted inside a gate
left by a philosopher
or a physicist, but I had
come to this, a woman
trapped by causalities
in the state of grief.

In a shroud of white noise
I lived for fifteen years,
and when I emerged
I saw the particle
my father studied
changed by the beam splitter—
had it gone through intact
or been caught by reflection?

The yard held pollen
and gnats. Two fruits swayed
on the apple-pear during a series
of moments in which
time appeared to be going
backwards. I held passion
at a distance. The sun beaded
on a plate, fried glass,
and changed overnight
into a different star, one
that cycled through spots
like an animal every eleven years.

Sun stroked the yard,
the hydrangea greened.
Children in the recess yard
became other child bodies
fused with age. I slept late,

mornings, and wakened
to their cries.

Field Thistle

Herb and spine,
the flat-fisted dream
of stars and dew
formed when he walked
with his telescope
through grasses spotted
by the spit bug.

A raucous noise,
the dawn of great beauty
and he with his tripod
matting the grasses as he walked.

I never saw him dead
on a bed of white down.
Never heard past
the death rattle,
and so, for me
he lives still
here in the ragged, noxious weeds
that make up North America.

He with his freely creeping root system,
milk-juiced,
the most persistent
of all my fathers
on arable lands.

Opalescence

That glass sagged as it aged
was a myth.
Glass was neither fluid nor solid,

borrowed from sand
and not to be given back.
We were reminded to look

at once opaque, tender, and nostalgic.
Possibly we'd be found out,
but only if comfort grew too precious.

In beeswax and copper,
lead or scissors,
the faeries might appear.

They would be different
than will o' the wisps.
Less slender, curves stuck between lead *cames*.

Mulch might catch fire,
manure steam,
but we must go on copying

the moon in its cordon,
carving the sun from opal
as day and night grew equal.

In each of us was a light box,
call it the soul. So we could transmit
the message of light, if not its substance.

Or we would darken to a cold stare
like a fish swaying close
to the surface of these egregious waters.

Dry Drunks

This morning they rose, showered and shaved,
      headed for the office en masse.
Trees white-knuckled the wind,

Canadian geese chased one another
      with the same honks as cars driven too fast
down slick roads.

They are clean and honest enough
      to pick up the dime
lying bare and symbolic in the street

and return it with a clink
      to a can. Behind the bistro
full bottles gleam blue, yellow, red,

primary as garden annuals, but it is meetings
      they attend, not bars.
If every so often one of them should forget

the denseness of knotted wood,
      dead leaves braiding clematis just now
unfolding against a trellis,

it would make no more difference
      than if Abraham had neglected
to honor his pact with God.

The long, slow days of sobriety march
      the way the ass does, with Isaac
on its back. Whether they intend it or not

sons and daughters will be sacrificed.
      Appointments never made will be kept,
and they'll return to dust-free houses.

Their wives—where are wives but in the kitchen—
    will watch olive oil burn
and sing a little in the pan, then add,

with wild abandon, all the flowers,
    trinkets, charms, flesh, and stones
an insatiable hunger has bestowed.

Sea Smoke

As far as winter
stretches, I am alone
on this cliff
staring down at what
could be fog or steam or mist.

The whisper of reeds recalls
a wound I barely remember,
a figure who could be...

As far as we are apart,
as old as that
and more, our differences,
the complaint you mustered
upon finding heat coalesced
into a lump.

The body, cremated, can be compressed
to diamonds. Stroke of gray
on a gull, prescience,
hull of the boat that might have saved Icarus
when he came of age...

As far as the dead are concerned,
the sun is smoke
the moon milk,
stars salt. With seared eyes
the dead see the living,
hunched figures
who find by dreaming
what it is they are looking for.

A glimpse of cloth,
bone of hanger left between a coat
torn from its closet

and the marred dowel
from which hung
garment bags. Mothballs
of ancient Styrofoam,
the insects have eaten
through silk, cashmere, linen,
and more.

Hat that should have been worn
in minus centigrade—
the dead see
our flesh in tatters
and the foreshortened days,
foreshadowing.

Monotone

Before you were born to color
there was another,
and this one held only form.

Light and darkness vied for their place.
Maybe you were aware of pallor,
a sameness of days, winter
stalks of pampas grass
alike in death as life.

The road was irrigated with cars, persons.
It held you tautly in its band,
and sometimes you wore out
that road in sleeplessness.
Then, in sickness
all the years of your life
blurred together.
Daylight held a few vague shapes
in its beak. There were no birds.

Before you were born
the world was full of insects
who sang by rubbing their legs together.

It could be said,
if passivity held sway,
you preferred not to enter
by a selvage
or cross any corners.

In this way you were perfectly honest.
You told no lies, even to yourself.
Cleaned glass each week with newspaper.

In time you came to see
the irresistible—what hue would it bear?
How could it be caught and tamed?
And were there any fruits
named after it?

New Poems

The Mirror of Wood

after Neruda

In the mirror of wood
are eyes, hair, a figure
who has lost her violin.

Amputations take place.
In the mirror of wood
there are strings and webs.

I am a woman so I sweep.
Sweep and rake wood and concrete,
my eyes on the sky

that drains, like a shell,
each hue from the color
of what was before.

In the mirror of wood
I see what has not been done.
Old scars, oaths, recriminations—

the earth is yellow with leaves.
Their veins, varicose, tip
and lilt when the rake

picks them up. I pull my hands
from the tines of the rake.
I put on my face.

I am a woman so I rake.
The sound is that of scratching,
not as a cat scratches

at the door to enter,
but as one who knocks
on the earth, finds it hollow,

and continues
to peer beneath its gleaming surface
for clouds, branches, and myths.

Montezuma's Revenge

What, after all, can be said
about the indelicate?
That it's a nasty business.
Mahi mahi under a palapa,
rice soaked in vanilla—
the rope bridge we crossed
to get from resort to culture
gave no sign of sickness.

What, after all, can be said
about revenge? That it is infectious.
I remember a sea the color of turquoise,
heavy birds with black feathers.
The waiter said,
We're out of chicken, I bring you pelican.
A slice of lime posed like a smile
on the lip of the largest glass I'd ever seen.

Bloated with pleasure, we walked the beach,
fended off vendors who only wanted
to feed their children.
Come here, spend your money,
one said to me. Quartz charms,
turquoise and silver, silver and malachite,
silver and onyx. Across the street,
scowling women hung their worn towels

like flags. The church, the Tequila Factory,
the darkness inside each shop
conveyed scents of musk,
wrinkled oranges, speckled bananas, cheap lipstick.
Was it the leg of a chicken
forgotten for hours at room temperature
or the nameless green pepper
that made our eyes tear, our throats beg

in another language
for the most essential element,
here where Montezuma still owns the water.

Heat Lightning

That to which we were beholden
as children. I remember the silent flicker
in clouds of gauze, how we,
banished to a closet-sized room,
lay flat-chested on iron bunks.

Voices outside. The scuttled car
returning a grown woman
to her home. The whole world desperate
and she, in heels,
clicked up the sidewalk and turned a key.

Maybe it was the mystery
of her womanhood, her fullness,
to be revealed with the next silent firework.
Or perhaps what the heat meant
was sweat, and sleeplessness.

It showed things as they were—
dishes crusted over,
pots black enough to take a flash of blue
when we snuck down
to the kitchen.

Each stroke of light dull as the moon
hidden behind the sheet
the woman would be lying under,
in her grown-up house joined to ours.
There the man would turn slightly

in his sleep, sensing her perfume, her lingerie,
imagining she had been out with *the girls*,
not bothering to wake or talk.
She, our mascot, magnet, compass rose,
might lie under the spell of idolatry for years.

So what if she never needed to tell the truth,
which was, after all, nothing more
than a blur, a white lie
leftover from a series of days
above ninety degrees.

Salt

after Webster's

Below the salt, there the poor live,
folks who have never seen white asparagus.
That which lends tang or piquancy, as in, wit—
the stockfish are barrel shaped today,
ringed with muscle and open at both ends...

Think of the severing—how an accident singes past
from present and is preserved,
the bathwater softened
with Epsom salts,
the saltcellar plunged in nightmare.
How rare nowadays to put oil in a well,
to distill, to scatter minerals
in order to deceive prospective buyers.

Above the salt, here sit the rich,
while the poor store or save,
see Matthew, 5:13.
Any person may be regarded as noble,
more or less honored depending upon
how far they stand
from the bowl of salt placed like a child's allowance
in the middle of the table.

Memory could be cathartic
if it were approached in an oyster-like fashion,
if the oyster hosted a crab, say,
built in to the soft burlesque body
like furniture. Suppose the crab crystallized—
its arachnid-like arms and legs
caught waving radically as an experienced sailor.

How biting the colloquial.
This fellow had weathered water dancing,

this one was accustomed to leaping—
saltation, a sudden variation in gait as the sea
came close to him, its mannerisms
reminiscent of salt grass.

How acidic to give false value to books and prices,
to alter a past that is only a flat, crisp cracker
with platitudes and Pollyanic sayings.
Rather say the ocean—the music, if you will,
is nightshade, has left its state and season
on account of cultivation.

Perennial, alkaline, ransacked of its fine meats
that were, before, plentiful
as paper, soap, and pulp.

Porch Light

It shines under slanting rain,
giving and taking back
the storms that welded Father
to his work, the kiss
that would pry him home.

In autumn we become raw
and damp-boned, the fungus
still eating like a cancer
into wood, the last chrysanthemum
poised to die, its creased black petals.

I like to think about what happens
under this light
so vague and soft. How
clouds scud. The promise
of a new moon that grows and disappears.

To think and wish
is an excess. I see leaves plastered
against the welcome mat, mounds of earth
a mole has left in faded grass.
The man comes home

or doesn't. Either way a woman
returns to her thread, the clamp
holding one flower to another,
the pins that keep her hair
in place.

Butter and Eggs

after a flower from the Snapdragon family

The shifting lips of snapdragon, too yellow,
grow like dreams.

How dense and vulgar breakfast is.

I had three children soft as butter,
their innards yolk-like.

When I woke I was a witch with creased cheeks.

The house was freshly painted—
no pleats disturbed French lace.

Eggs sputtered in a pan.

The sun had burned grasses beside the freeway,
and, in patches, certain trees turned copper.

I woke to an empty house—don't say *nest*.

I meant to walk into town but that was common.

The toad in the children's pool deforms itself
trying to escape. Rózsa holds it to her flat chest.
She might be the granddaughter of a friend…

Lips of snapdragon, dreams sour with age,
reparations from my spiked tongue.

A bit of mail is delivered by a white truck
flinging its shadow like an envelope.

It might be the sun, well past middle-age.

If lace trembles and undulates,
what was meant to be delicious is done.

The Family Goat

We like to love him despite the smell
of his goatishness. On good days
he stands on top of the makeshift house
and roars. On bad days he has eaten

whatever it was we were saving for ourselves.
This could be indicative of a certain
obstreperousness—his tendency
to act like a child with the horns

that need rubbing, yet can be rubbed
the wrong way. When we bleed
as a result of flaying him with our words
the blood runs dark and wet, not

orange and dry like Christ's.
We like to say *he should know better*
even when our condition has never been worse.
He is happy to goad us, to become

ever more goat-like, to sleep in the green swath
between the shed and the masterpiece
that was once our home. There a moon came
and went, a scentless object no one could touch

until the night he refused the solace of escape,
and tore certain objets d'art from the walls.
Unlike the elephant who occupied
our closet, with its spit of a tail, this goat

was unable to accept our feverish
attempts at affection. Cowed
but never cowering, he hid in corners
frayed by wear. His misdeeds multiplied.

As if it were not enough merely to sulk,
to be stuck with relentless germs, wills, and years,
we squandered our best stores on him.
He remained obstinate, unruly

in his refusal to take on the role of middle child,
father, husband. More like death
than any person, he continues to eat his way
through the holes in our memories.

Echocardiogram

My heart is a herd of horses
streaming toward the finish line,
hooves smacking against the track.

My heart is ill, swollen in its chambers
where once the virus came and made me believe
in Kierkegaard's *Either/Or*.

Scaffolding on the cot where I listen
to the dark blood that will not clot running
smoothly through aorta and artery. My pulse

runs amok. One hundred beats
per minute the shy technician says as he replaces
that part of the bed that let my left breast drop,

apologizes for what he will do next—
locate my heart between slots of rib.
Smooth as jelly the minutes pass.

I listen to these horses grown more fantastic
with each jolt of the whip from the small jockey
who has lost so much weight

only denial will keep her here.

The Glass Chicken

Perhaps because it is more artifice than art
we are attracted to it, hungry
for what it represents—
this chicken with a price tag.

Appetites being expensive, manners aside,
the chicken rules the shop
where fluted objets d'art proliferate.
This hen is a queen.

Never dirty, not in danger—
for there are no dogs here.
This is a life of privilege. Poverty forgotten,
the glass chicken sits in the window.

Hollow insides, made in the glory hole,
that word obscene, full of connotation.
Are we in awe as the fire rages
inside the oven where this chicken

cooked with no aroma, no gizzard nor liver,
its substance arcane?
Must we admit the muse, a feather plucked
and clucked over,

a bit of bloodied meat chased with its head cut off
around the dull yard
grown now cold and hard
and tough as memory.

Confessional

I would have wanted to escape my body had it not

    yet been perfected.

You can work in a space the size of a closet,

    the teacher said.

No way to make sense of day and night apart from

    this that was mine.

My leg swung back and forth across a wood floor

    in a master class.

My leg was praised and learned to rise and fall

    apart from me.

My arms grew heavy because I willed them to.

The swinging taught me how to give back what

    could have been.

It must be growing late if the hour's round and fat

    as the moon.

The Gray Trees of August

Float in their dry beds
as if someone had died.
Someone has died.
Outside the pharmacy

they have removed the plants,
even the last blueberry
that stood over its pot gesticulating
as it browned.

The gray trees wandered all night
in their places. Sleep didn't come.
Where there might have been tetanus
a deep muscle ached in a woman's arm.

Pewter in the trees,
lead in the sky,
clouds where rain happens
before it can reach the earth.

In dust and pills a few pages
of the book that will be winter
loosens its little coat, removes
its illusions.

As if someone had died,
all night the trees stood still
for a Shiva attended by no one.
Heavy casseroles clattered as glass lids

sat upside down.
Countertops and floors sprouted
more of the gray dirt
a woman might wipe with her cloth.

A few stars cooled
as they rusted to the sky
and stuck fast. At five a.m.,
before sleep, came morning.

The woman thought of her heart.
Maybe she wandered outside herself,
beside wild roses gray as the trees.
Like treacle, what was left of the creek oozed.

Gossip

It began as this and that,
spread like phlox and impatiens.
Whispers, thistles, corncobs
strewn beside the road.
Nothing could be the same after *he said,*
she said, no one would come
unannounced up the long driveway
paved in broken glass.

It began as a descent
to a place that could not be read,
like Gertrude Stein's *The Making of Americans.*
Just a start, a green innocence.
Suppose an affair, an intrigue
held on the tongue,
a slice of lemon or lime.

The end will be bitter—
make no mistake, but the beginning's sweet.
Because no one's the wiser,
no one listens or cares
when the women gather in twos and threes,
sweat on their necks
dried to crystals so minute
they would have to be tasted to be told.

What sense could be made of words?
A mesh bag for lingerie.
Sour cherries, white trash.
Insistence. A half moon. A phrase
of jazz, the sheets swaying on a line
where once upon a time linens were fresh
and even the most ordinary day
sparkled with sin.

Cobblestone Streets

Made for trouble,
meant to slow things down.
Narrow alleys,
lines of laundry to reel in,
a language smelling of garlic and gutturals.
Colors, scents, and secrets.
The street will not tell,
the map will not get you found.

These cars, these houses—
look now, none of them are yours.
Admit you are lost.
That you came from Europe
and can't remember when or why.
Perhaps there was a war.
A girl, barely a woman,
smiled at a man.

Skimpy clothes were thrown down,
right there, on the stones.
The moon was slim.
The earth was a flat plate, an offering
still full of fish and Tarsiers.
Someone had died of drink.
A pillar of stones for memory,
flowers piled in a cairn.

Silk

From the cocoon of the worm,
from the prim silk blouse,

all that shines in corn cobs
and contains seeds of luster.

After I lost the green fodder
of my sleep I wanted to parachute

from my ungainly dreams,
away from doves folded on wires,

and all I had earned—ambition,
that stagnant balloon,

lay fixed around my knees.
The money tree purpled in autumn.

A woman outlined her divorce.
Here and there certain webs

were ruined, as, from the spider,
came more of what could not be sold,

destroyed, or given away.
From the prison of a week awake

I walked, feeling my way
past the silent doves,

the uniforms, the counsel of friends,
birthdays, seasons, and cancers.

Birth in the sheen of ugliness.
Death in the conversation of an old man's hand,

Sidney Bloom, who gestured, upon being told
he'd meet his dead wife in heaven,

enough already.

Magpie Eyes

Whatever shines
or is lost like the moon,
that yellow—

a glint of nostalgia, the train
in passing, the bells and cars,
what I want is not that.

All I've seen
is dark as obsidian,
friable as sodalite.

From Brazil came cross-sections of geode.
From my parents came arithmetic,
algebra, parameters.

From a studio of kitsch
I gunny-sacked diagonal tulips
and bridge spans.

Whatever shone I befriended—
coins, diamonds, strands of pearls
cultured in fresh water, salt water.

The world was plural.
I bought a *bouclé* coat in winter white.
What I saw was what I needed.

There wasn't time for sleep.
Debt rose like water.
My husband, the collector,

slipped away from me
clutching a pillar, his eyes
blue-green.

I think it was in peace time he left,
and then it was yesterday,
the year of war

and wooden nickels.
One by one my charms grew legs:
quartz elephant, horse, owl, turtle

moving slowly as the earth.
That's when I took my butterfly net
and walked on up the ridge.

I can't tell you what I caught there.
It was rare
but not popular enough to keep.

NOTES

"Beethoven and the Birds" was inspired by a line from Beethoven's letter to his doctor friend Wegeler, written in 1801: "...for two years I have avoided almost all social gatherings because it is impossible for me to say to people: 'I am deaf.'"

"Tic Douloureux" (*Storm*) means *painful twitch* and refers to trigeminal neuralgia.

Oradourian Gold (*Circe's Island*) refers to the history of a town "Oradour sur Glane" in the Périgueux region of France that was destroyed on a sunny June day towards the end of WWII; its five hundred citizens massacred by fire. It is now a memorial ground. What remains are a few stone walls, sewing machines and chunks of metal that didn't burn. Arguments have been made that the German soldiers were seeking Nazi gold suspected to be buried in the village of Oradour. No gold was found (Mackness, Robin. *Massacre at Oradour*. Random House: New York, 1988.)

The poems from *Latticework* were inspired by a collaboration with fiber artist Erika Carter. Several poems are included in Contemporary Quiltart Visual Verse Project in conjunction with Carter's "Time Series."

Cat's Paw is a type of glass that contains ring mottles, or small circular patterns of opacity, on its surface.

Cames (*Opalescence*) refers to a network of lead soldered at every joint.

ACKNOWLEDGEMENTS

Thanks to the following presses for publishing these books, from which poems have been excerpted for this volume:

"Worship of the Visible Spectrum," *Breitenbush Books*, 1988

"Beethoven and the Birds," *Blue Begonia Press*, 1996

"Storm," *Blue Begonia Press*, 1998

"Red Town," *Silverfish Review Press*, 2001

"Circe's Island," *Silverfish Review Press*, 2003

"Latticework," *David Robert Books*, 2004

"Opalescence," *David Robert Books*, 2005

New Poems have appeared as follows:

Illya's Honey, "Magpie Eyes"; *FIELD*, "Heat Lightning"; *Literary Imagination*, "The Mirror of Wood"; *Mankato Poetry Journal*, "Porchlight"; *Journal of the American Medical Association (JAMA)*, "Montezuma's Revenge" and "Echocardiogram"; *Tattoo Highway*, "The Glass Chicken" and "The Gray Trees of August"; *poemmemoirstory*, "Butter and Eggs"; *Northwest Review*, "The Family Goat."

The following anthologies reprinted these poems:

"Magpie Eyes," "The Family Goat" and "Heat Lightning" appeared in *Weathered Pages: Poems from the Pole*, Blue Begonia Press, 2005.

"Asylum" and "Sad Breed" also appeared in the *Prairie Schooner Anthology of Jewish American Writers*, 1998.

"Tinnitus" was included in JAMA's Anthology *Uncharted Lines*, 1998, edited by Charlene Breedlove.

"The Duty of Ideas" and "Lilacs" appeared in *March Hares, The Best Poems of Fine Madness 1982-2002*.

I am deeply indebted to my family—Tom, Drew, Jocelyn, Lisa, and Josh.

To editor Jim Bodeen for his sense of purpose in the art of writing.

To my friends Anne Pitkin, Joannie Kervran Stangeland, Susan Lane, Darby Ringer, Eileen Duncan—*Young Poets* all.

Thanks to Barbara L. Thomas for her friendship, and to textile artist Erika Carter for inspiration.

Thanks to my fellow co-editors at *Fine Madness*: Sean Bentley, David Edelman, John Malek, and Anne Pitkin.

Finally, my gratitude to my mother, Dr. Bernice Bloom Kastner, for her unflagging support of my writing.

A Note about the Author

Judith Skillman is the winner of numerous awards, including the Eric Mathieu King Fund Award from the Academy of American Poets. She has held artist residencies at Port Townsend from the Centrum Foundation. In 1994 the King County Arts Commission awarded her a public arts grant; her poem is etched in the windows of the Kent Regional Justice Center.

She was the recipient of a Writer's Fellowship from the Washington State Arts Commission in 1991. She also received the King County Arts Commission Publication Prize Award in 1987, judged by Madeline DeFrees. In 2001 her book "Red Town," published by Silverfish Review Press, was a finalist in the Washington Center for the Book Award Contest.

Skillman's poems have appeared in *FIELD, Poetry, Northwest Review, Prairie Schooner, The Iowa Review, Southern Review, Journal of the American Medical Association (JAMA), Seneca Review,* and many other journals. Her collaborative translations of French-Belgian poet Anne-Marie Derèse have been published by *Northwest Review* and BEACONS. She has been a co-editor of *Fine Madness* since 2000.

Skillman holds an M.A. in English Literature from the University of Maryland, and has done graduate work in Comparative Literature and Translation Studies at the University of Washington. She is a faculty member of City University in Bellevue, Washington.

green press
INITIATIVE

Colophon

The text and display types of this edition are set in Adobe Jenson, a faithful electronic version of the 1470 roman face of Nicolas Jenson. Jenson was a Frenchman, employed as the mintmaster at Tours. Legend has it that he was sent to Mainz in 1458 by Charles VII to learn the new art of printing in the shop of Gutenberg, and import it to France. But he never returned, next appearing in Venice in 1468. Type historian Daniel Berkeley Updike praises the Jenson Roman for "its readability, its mellowness of form, and the evenness of color in mass." Updike concludes, "Jenson's roman types have been the accepted models for roman letters ever since he made them, and, repeatedly copied in our own day, have never been equalled." The cover font is Mrs. Eaves, designed by Zuzana Licko, Émigré Fonts, and is a historical revival based on the design of Baskerville. Mrs. Eaves was John Baskerville's helper and housekeeper.

Cover design by Valerie Brewster, Scribe Typography.
Text design by Rodger Moody and Connie Kudura, ProtoType Graphics.
Printed on acid-free papers and bound by Thomson-Shore, Inc.